Preacher

Preacher

The Wit and Wisdom of Reverend Will B. Dunn

by Doug Marlette

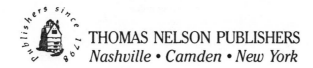

Publishers since 1798

THOMAS NELSON PUBLISHERS
Nashville • Camden • New York

To

Melinda

REVEREND DUNN, I'VE ASKED YOU HERE TO SEE IF YOU'D CONSIDER WRITING AN ADVICE COLUMN FOR THE "BUGLE.."

..AFTER ALL, YOU ARE AN EXPERT IN HUMAN RELATIONS!...

BUT... BUT I'M JUST A SIMPLE COUNTRY PREACHER! WHAT DO I KNOW ABOUT THE MEDIA?

MARIETTE

YOU'RE TOO MODEST, REVEREND... WHAT WOULD IT TAKE TO PERSUADE YOU TO DO IT?...

TEN CENTS PER WORD, EIGHT INCHES ON THE LOCAL FRONT, TWELVE-POINT BOLD-FACE BYLINE, PAGE ONE PROMO AND PLAY ABOVE THE FOLD!...

DID YOU DECIDE TO DO THAT ADVICE COLUMN FOR THE "BUGLE", PREACHER?

WELL, NOW, SON, THAT'S REALLY NOT MY CALLIN'...

BUT YOU SHOULD, PREACHER! REALLY!... YOU'D BE WONDERFUL!

AW, HUSH...

MARIETTE

C'MON, PREACHER, YOU SHOULDN'T HIDE YOUR LIGHT UNDER A BUSHEL! GO AHEAD AND WRITE IT!...

OH, I DUNNO...

"PEARLS FROM THE PULPIT!"

Dear Preacher,
I am not the kind of person who usually writes letters to advice Columnists...

but now, it seems, all of that has changed.
Sincerely,
Lew Powell

MARLETTE

Dear Preacher,
You are a mealy-mouthed, CHICKEN-LIVERED COWARD.

YOU NEVER TAKE A STAND ON ANYTHING. YOU'RE AFRAID TO BE HELD ACCOUNTABLE FOR YOUR OPINION.

YOU LACK THE GUTS TO TAKE RESPONSIBIL-ITY FOR WHAT YOU BELIEVE. WELL, I SAY "PUT UP OR SHUT UP!"
Sincerely,

MARLETTE

ANONYMOUS

Dear Preacher,
I have fears too numerous to mention. I am afraid of everything.

This is excruciatingly painful. I need someone who will counsel me with sensitivity and understanding.

Can you help?
Frightened

Dear Scaredy Cat,

Dear Preacher,
Your column sounds like it is written by a seven year old.

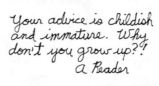

Your advice is childish and immature. Why don't you grow up?!
A Reader

Dear Reader,
Liar, Liar, Pants on fire!

DEAR Preacher,
I know you'll
understand.

I Like to dress
up my microwave
IN women's
Lingerie.

Am I NORMAL?

WONDERING

MARIETTE

Dear Wondering,
What makes
you think I'll
understand?!

Dear Preacher,
My twin sister and I
think you are a phony.

There are enough so-called
"experts" making a fast buck
off of other people's problems
without you sticking your
big nose in where it doesn't belong!
What do you say to that?

MARIETTE

Dear Abby,

© Jefferson Communications, Inc. 1983
Distributed by Tribune Company Syndicate, Inc.

BEIN' A MINISTER MUST BE REALLY HARD, HUH, PREACHER?!

I MEAN, LIVING FOR OTHERS, LEADING AN EXEMPLARY LIFE! THAT'S A LOT OF RESPONSIBILITY! THE PRESSURES MUST BE TREMENDOUS!

HAVING TO SET A GOOD EXAMPLE!... PEOPLE WATCHING, WAITING FOR ONE FALSE MOVE, ONE SIGN OF HUMAN FRAILTY THEY CAN JUMP ON!... I DON'T KNOW HOW YOU HANDLE IT!...

I STAY HOME A LOT.

Y'KNOW, IN MY PROFESSION YOU HEAR A LOT ABOUT THE POOR AND DOWN-TRODDEN!... BUT, BY GOLLY, THE MATERIALLY BLESSED HAVE THEIR SPIRITUAL PROBLEMS, TOO!

THE FABULOUSLY WELL-TO-DO NEED MINISTERING TO AS MUCH AS ANYBODY ELSE!...

I RECKON.

IT'S A DIRTY JOB BUT SOMEBODY HAS TO DO IT!...

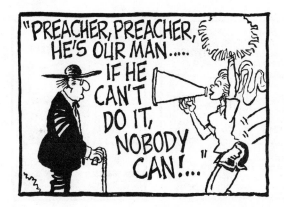

SURE, YOU'RE A VERY SUCCESSFUL BUSINESS TYCOON, BROTHER TADSWORTH, BUT ISN'T IT TROUBLING TO YOU WHEN YOU FORECLOSE ON WIDOWS AND ORPHANS?...

...ISN'T IT TROUBLING WHEN YOU CHEAT LOYAL EMPLOYEES?...

ISN'T IT TROUBLING WHEN YOU DOUBLECROSS FRIENDS AND BLACKMAIL COMPETITORS?!...

NO—WHAT'S TROUBLING ABOUT IT?

WHAT'S TROUBLING IS IT'S NOT TROUBLING!...

PREACHER DUNN, I LIKE YOU! YOU'RE MY KIND OF REVEREND! YOU KEEP YOUR MOUTH SHUT AND MIND YOUR OWN BUSINESS.

HOW WOULD YOU LIKE TO JOIN MRS. TADSWORTH AND ME AT THE CLUB FOR SUNDAY BRUNCH? SAY, ELEVEN O'CLOCK?...

WELL... OF COURSE, I HAVE MY SERVICE TO PREACH!...

CANCEL IT!

DON'T TELL ME, LORD!... LET ME GUESS!... THIS IS A TEST, RIGHT?

BROTHER TADSWORTH, SURELY YOU MUST FEEL JUST A BIT OF GUILT ABOUT THIS ITEM HERE WHERE YOU TRIED TO FORCE THE LITTLE OLD LADY TO SELL YOU HER PROPERTY...

.. TELLING HER SHE HAD TO EVACUATE BECAUSE AN EARTHQUAKE WAS PREDICTED; BULLDOZING HER HOME WHILE SHE WAS OUT, THEN OFFERING TO BUY IT FOR A FRACTION OF ITS WORTH!...

MARLETTE

BUSINESS IS BUSINESS!

BUT YOUR OWN GRANDMOTHER!...

Y'KNOW, I DID FEEL KINDA BAD ABOUT THAT LATER!...

NOW WE'RE GETTIN' SOMEWHERE!

I CAN'T LIVE WITH THE COMPROMISES I HAVE TO MAKE AS BIG BUBBA TADSWORTH'S CORPORATE CONSCIENCE — CLOSING MY EYES TO HIS ETHICAL INSENSITIVITIES!...

TADSWORTH

I CAN'T SERVE ANOTHER MINUTE AS SPIRITUAL RUBBER STAMP FOR HIS ROBBER BARON SCRUPLES!...

BROTHER TADSWORTH, I WANT TO TALK TO YOU!

PREACHER DUNN!...JUST THE MAN I WANT TO SEE! I LIKE THE WAY YOU'VE BEEN SEEN AND NOT HEARD AROUND HERE! I'M DOUBLING YOUR SALARY!

MARLETTE

..THEN AGAIN, YOU CAN'T DO ANY GOOD UNLESS YOU WORK WITHIN THE SYSTEM!

B. TADSWORTH

Dear Preacher,
I have trouble making a decision and sticking to it.

My friends and family are fed up with me.

Can I overcome my indecisiveness?
Wishy-washy

Dear Wishy-washy,
Maybe.
Maybe not.

MARLETTE

Dear Preacher,
I am sick of these T.V. evangelists making millions off of their gullible viewers.

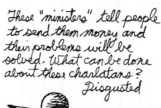

These "ministers" tell people to send them money and their problems will be solved. What can be done about these charlatans?
Disgusted

Dear Disgusted,
For solutions to these and other problems just send in a donation to me by check or money order c/o this newspaper.

MARLETTE

Dear Preacher,
My father's a convict. My mother's insane. My sister's on drugs and I think I'm a train.

What do you think about that?
Choo-choo

Dear Choo-choo,
I give it a ninety-five. It's got a good beat and it's easy to dance to.

I SEE THIS ADVICE COLUMN AS A CHANCE TO BRING MY THEOLOGICAL INSIGHT AND YEARS OF EXPERIENCE IN HUMAN RELATIONS TO BEAR ON THE GREAT ETHICAL ISSUES OF OUR TIME!...

Dear Preacher,
Our family is torn with strife and dissension.

Will you settle this argument which has caused us so much pain and grief?

Should we watch "Bonanza" re-runs or "Bowling for Dollars"?

REVEREND DUNN — I NEED YOU TO RUN SOME INTERFERENCE FOR ME INVOLVING A — UM — PERSONAL MATTER.

BROTHER TADSWORTH, HUMAN RELATIONS IS MY BUSINESS.

GOOD.... GOOD.... I KNEW I COULD COUNT ON YOU!

REVEREND DUNN, THIS IS MY SON, TAD — I WANT TO PUT TAD UP FOR ADOPTION!...

FATHER, THAT'S ILLEGAL.

UH — BROTHER TADSWORTH, PERHAPS THE BOY SHOULDN'T BE IN ON THIS CONVERSATION!...

IT'S ALL RIGHT!... WE'RE ALL ADULTS HERE!

BROTHER TADSWORTH, (HEH-HEH!) YOU CAN'T PUT YOUR OWN SON UP FOR ADOPTION!...

I'M SORRY, BUT HE JUST HASN'T WORKED OUT!

I WANT YOU TO TAKE CARE OF THE DETAILS, REVEREND....

BUT... BUT THAT'S IMMORAL!

Y'KNOW, REVEREND DUNN, I'VE BEEN THINKING OF DONATING A NEW WING TO THAT LITTLE OL' CHURCH BUILDING OF YOURS!....

ACTUALLY, BOY, THERE ARE THINGS LOTS WORSE THAN BEING AN ORPHAN....

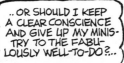

Dear Preacher,
Hey, you're a beautiful cat! No, I mean that sincerely.....

You're a marvelous columnist and a great human being in your own right.
Peace and Love

Dear Sammy Davis, Jr.,

Dear Preacher,
Nobody treats me as an individual.

I feel like a nameless, faceless non-entity, undifferentiated from the mass of humanity.

I want to feel like a distinct human being with unique finger prints and a specific identity. Any suggestions?
Somebody

To whom it may concern,

UH-OH!... MORE HATE MAIL....

Dear Alleged Human Being, You are a lousy little creep. I know where you live and I'm coming over to your house and punch you in the nose.

MARLETTE

THESE THREATENING LETTERS ARE ALWAYS THE SAME.... THE LITTLE COWARD PROBABLY DIDN'T EVEN SIGN HIS NAME!...

Please find enclosed my name, address, social security number and references.

WITH HATE MAIL IT'S NOT SO MUCH WHAT PEOPLE SAY.....

.... IT'S HOW THEY SAY IT!

MARLETTE

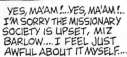

PREACHER, MAYBE MY PROBLEM IS THAT I'M A LATE BLOOMER!...

COULD BE!... SOME FOLKS TAKE A LITTLE LONGER THAN OTHERS TO REALIZE THEIR FULL POTENTIAL!... BUT THEY BLOOM SOONER OR LATER!...

REALLY, PREACHER?! DO YOU REALLY THINK I'LL BLOOM SOMEDAY?!...

'COURSE, IT'S ONLY A MATTER OF TIME BEFORE THEY FADE AND ROT!...

WHEN I'M FEELIN' LOW-DOWN AND POORLY, KUDZU, I LIKE TO READ THE STORY OF **JOB** AND HIS COUNTLESS HARDSHIPS, TRIALS AND TRIBULATIONS...

YOU MEAN YOU'RE UPLIFTED BY HIS EXAMPLE OF FAITH IN THE FACE OF UNENDURABLE SUFFERING?...

NAW—I JUST LIKE TO READ ABOUT FOLKS WORSE OFF THAN I AM!

PREACHER, WHAT'S THE SECRET TO CHEWIN' TOBACCO?...

AIN'T NO SECRET!...

MARLETTE

YOU JUST CHEW A PLUG 'TIL IT'S NICE AN' JUICY!...

CHEW IT UP GOOD NOW!... THAT'S RIGHT!

GULP!

WHICH BRINGS ME TO AN IMPORTANT POINT— NEVER SWALLOW!...

PREACHER, MY MAMA'S WORRIED SICK ABOUT ME!... SHE'S AFRAID I'VE FALLEN IN WITH A BAD CROWD!...

WELL NOW, THAT'S A LEGITIMATE MOTHERLY CONCERN!... JUST WHO IS THIS BAD CROWD UNDER WHOSE INFLUENCE SHE FEARS YOU'VE FALLEN?

MARLETTE

YOU.

Dear Preacher,
I feel totally
alienated from other
people....

....and that nobody
is able to under-
stand me or empathize
with my feelings....

....Do you know what
I mean?
Estranged

Dear Estranged,
No.

Dear Preacher,
I can't stop
crying. I guess I'm
just a very sensitive
person but I weep
over anything.

I take everything
personally— a harsh
word, a rude gesture.
Please help me.

I need sympathetic
understanding from a
sensitive counselor
who will gently help
me overcome this problem.
That's why I'm writing
to you.
Choked Up

Dear Crybaby,

Dear Preacher,
I am mortgaged to
the hilt. I owe
thousands of dollars
in gambling debts.

The mob is after
me. My wife is
threatening to leave
me. My own brother
has sworn out a
warrant for my arrest.

The bank is repos-
sessing my car.
You're my last
resort.
　　　Worried

Dear Worried,
　Boy, am I glad
I'm not in your
shoes!

Dear Preacher,
　I have a tendency to
over-react to things.
I make mountains out
of mole-hills.

Is there any
solution to my problem?
　　　Hysterical

Dear Hysterical,
　Simple. Change your
name, get plastic
surgery and move to
Tahiti.